UNDERSTA

LEARN2LEAD

Learn2Lead
© FIEC / The Good Book Company Ltd, 2007

The Good Book Company
Elm House, 37 Elm Road, New Malden, Surrey KT3 3HB, UK
Tel: 0845-225-0880
Fax: 0845-225-0990
Email: admin@thegoodbook.co.uk
Internet: www.thegoodbook.co.uk

Unless indicated, all Scripture references are taken from the HOLY BIBLE, NEW INTERNATIONAL VERSION. Copyright © 1973, 1978, 1984 International Bible Society. Used by permission.

ISBN 13: 978 1905564712

All rights reserved. Except as may be permitted by the Copyright Act, no part of this publication may be reproduced in any form or by any means without prior permission from the publisher.

Printed in India

LEARN2LEAD

TRACK 2
UNDERSTANDING DOCTRINE

WELCOME

Welcome to the *Understanding Doctrine* track of the *Learn2Lead* course – part of the local-church leadership training programme initially developed by the Fellowship of Independent Evangelical Churches. We hope you find this course both enjoyable and useful to your life and ministry.

It is likely that you will be using this book as part of a group within your congregation. But it is also possible to work through this material alone. Whichever method applies to you, we would encourage you to work prayerfully and diligently through the material, taking every opportunity to discuss the work with Christians around you.

CONTENTS

TRACK 2

UNDERSTANDING DOCTRINE

	PREFACE	6
2.1	GOD His being	11
2.2	GOD His character	16
2.3	THE BIBLE	21
2.4	THE LORD JESUS CHRIST His person	25
2.5	THE LORD JESUS CHRIST His death	30
2.6	THE LORD JESUS CHRIST His resurrection and reign	35
2.7	THE HOLY SPIRIT	40
2.8	THE HUMAN RACE	45
2.9	THE CHURCH	50
2.10	THE FUTURE	55

PREFACE

'THE THINGS YOU HAVE HEARD me say in the presence of many witnesses entrust to reliable men who will also be qualified to teach others' (2 Timothy 2:2)

Developing leaders in the church is the purpose of *Learn2Lead*. Leadership of the body of Christ is important, and therefore taking time to develop the leaders of the future is a vital aspect of building up God's church.

LEADERSHIP IS THE KEY

If you asked your Christian friends to sum up their feelings about contemporary church life, two of the words that would crop up most frequently might well be *frustration* and *disappointment*. How can that be? It's not because there's anything wrong with the gospel. That is still the power of God for the salvation of everyone who believes in the Lord Jesus Christ. It may be something to do with the way we do church. God has given us all the resources we need to fulfil his plans for this generation, but there is a crying need to discover, nurture, train and liberate the ministries of people within the church. And that means competent and effective leadership.

CHANGING THE CULTURE

Many of us come from a background where everyone expected the Minister to do everything – except perhaps play the organ, teach Sunday School or make the tea. And more disturbingly, the Minister expected it to be that way too. The vision for *Learn2Lead* is to create a culture where everyone in the church – especially young people – see leadership as something they aspire to. When Paul wrote to Timothy, he obviously expected that there would be people in the church who wanted to be leaders. We want people in the church to see their leaders at work and say, 'Under God, I'd love to be able to do that!'

WHAT IS LEARN2LEAD?

Learn2Lead is an introductory course for church members who are not in a position to take time off work for more preparation for their role as leaders. It draws on the experience of the team that already trains people through a residential and placement programme called *Prepared for Service*. When you have completed *Learn2Lead* you may consider further study under the *Prepared for Service* programme or alternatively, with the Open Bible Institute. Details of these organisations can be found at the end of this workbook.

WHO TEACHES LEARN2LEAD?

The Scriptures indicate that those who are already doing important work in the church have it as their responsibility to train others to carry forward the work. The apostle Paul told his son in the faith, Timothy, 'The things you have heard me say in the presence of many witnesses entrust to reliable men who will also be qualified to teach others' (2 Timothy 2:2).

Learn2Lead is a tool for experienced leaders to use to teach others. It is designed to help those 'at the helm' to assist a new generation of leaders as they learn how to lead others. Tutors will normally be church leaders and others whose ministry has earned the respect and confidence of those they lead.

WHO MARKS LEARN2LEAD?

Learn2Lead is a course designed for use within your congregation under the guidance of your church leader. Their feedback is going to be the most beneficial to you as they know you as a person and see your ministry in action. However, you may also like an independent person to look at your work, mark it and (if successful) issue you with a certificate that acknowledges your many hours of study. If this is the case then you are welcome to submit a folder of your work (containing answers to each of the exercises in this book) to the Open Bible Institute. For full details (including the current marking fee) please see the website: *www.open-bible-institute.org*.

WHO IS LEARN2LEAD FOR?

It is for everyone in the local church who has the potential to be a leader. And the definition of leadership? That quality that makes other people want to follow you. You may be in leadership already as an elder or youth work co-ordinator. Perhaps people in the church have suggested that you have the leadership gifts that could be developed for the future. *Learn2Lead* is not just for potential church leaders, it is also hoped that it will assist any church member who is given responsibility in the church.

FIVE TRACKS

Learn2Lead consists of five tracks of training looking at the knowledge, skills and attitudes required to be developed by leaders in the church.

Understanding the Bible, Understanding Doctrine, Understanding Leadership, Leadership in Practice 1 and Leadership in Practice 2

THREE ELEMENTS TO THE COURSE

There are three elements to the course:
1. **Individual study** – this should be done before meeting with your tutor and the group.
2. **Group session** – this would normally include a review of individual study; discussion of some of the answers; review of any action points from the previous group session and preview of the next unit to be studied etc.
3. **Ministry opportunity** – there may be ways in which the study material from the unit can be implemented in your own ministry.

So *Learn2Lead* is not just about gathering information and getting the answers right but also applying that information so that you learn by experience in the church.

THE TOOLS YOU WILL NEED

- **Bible** – *Learn2Lead* uses the NIV Bible throughout.

- **Notebook** – You will need to make a record of your answers to questions and other notes and we suggest you have a notebook which you can use in conjunction with this student manual. At the end of these ten units, there is the option to submit the work you have done for marking by the Open Bible Institute. All students who submit work of an appropriate standard will be issued with a certificate. If you would like to work towards this certificate, please keep all your answers to the unit questions in your notebook. Once you have finished unit 10, neat versions of your answers can be submitted to the Open Bible Institute with the appropriate marking fee.

- **Bible Dictionary** – It would be useful for you to have access to a good Bible Dictionary. Student discounts are available through the Open Bible Institute office.

THE SYMBOLS

- The Bible passages by this symbol must be read. There are also a number of other references which should be looked at if you have time.

- These questions are designed to be worked through on your own and usually have factual answers.

- These questions are designed for discussion during your group meeting. Come prepared with some ideas.

- The six Old Testament units from Understanding the Bible have questions with this symbol. They are important as they show the 'big picture' of what God planned and did through Jesus Christ throughout history.

- These are points of application and further work which will help you to develop what you have learned in the unit.

The value of *Learn2Lead* is not only found in the quality of the material but particularly in its application. This is the secret of effective leadership in the body of Christ. The *Learn2Lead* team are interested in ensuring that the words contained within this book come alive in your role of leadership and in the church as a whole. If you can help us develop the material to ensure that this continues to happen please contact us, we would love to hear how you are progressing.

Remember leadership is action – never just a position!

Learn2Lead c/o The Good Book Company,
Elm House, 37 Elm Road, New Malden, Surrey KT3 3HB, UK
For further information please also see the FIEC website: www.fiec.org.uk

UNIT 2.1

GOD

His being

Hear, O Israel: The LORD our God, the LORD is one. Love the Lord your God with all your heart and with all your soul and with all your strength. **Deuteronomy 6:4,5**

THE BIBLE, being written for all people everywhere, assumes the existence of God. We only have to use our eyes to know that there is a supreme being to whom we are accountable (Romans 1:19,20). Even in the West today when, exceptionally, atheism has become an option, the vast majority of people say they believe in God. The question then becomes, in the words of the title of a recent book, *When you say 'God', what do you mean?* Very often it is a 'god' of people's own invention. The mistake that many people make when they come to think about God is the one that people have always made.

UNIT 2.1

A. THE GLORY OF GOD

 Read Psalm 50:21 and Romans 1:22-23

 What is the mistake, pointed out by God himself in these verses?

The problem of idolatry – of making up our own image of God – is that we limit and belittle him, when we were made to glorify him (Isaiah 43:7, Romans 1:21ff).

 Look at these passages...
- Exodus 33:18-23
- Luke 2:9,14
- John 1:14
- Revelation 4:11; 14:7; 1:12-18

 From these verses, what do you understand by the glory of God? What a concept! You will need several answers.

God's glory is something he is not prepared to share with anyone else (Isaiah 42:8). So John's statement that *We have seen his glory, the glory of the Only Begotten, who came from the Father, full of grace and truth* (John 1:14) comes with explosive force and leads us into the Christian doctrine of the Trinity. In the words of the FIEC doctrinal basis...

There is one God, who exists eternally in three distinct but equal persons: the Father, the Son and the Holy Spirit.

This explains how God can know and express love within his own person – he enjoys fellowship within himself. It means that we, moral creatures made in his image, can only find fullness of life within that same kind of fellowship – with others certainly, but supremely with God himself (1 John 1:1-4).

B. THE TRINITY

The doctrine of the Trinity affirms key truths about God:
- there is only one God
- God is one (unity)
- the Father is God
- the Son is God
- the Spirit is God
- the Father is neither the Son nor the Spirit
- the Son is not the Spirit.

The doctrine of the Trinity is revealed progressively in Scripture.

UNIT 2.1

 Read Deuteronomy 6:4-5

This is the creed God gave to his people in the Old Testament. What was the first thing they needed to learn about God?

However, even the Hebrew word used here for *one* can have the connotation of *unity*. It is also used, for example, of God's institution of marriage in Genesis 2:24 where God says the man and his wife will become *one flesh*.

As the Old Testament moves on, there are many hints that God is one and yet more than one at the same time. The strongest clue from the Old Testament is that someone is coming on a very special mission… someone who will rescue God's people from their enemies.

 Read Isaiah 9:6

Isaiah gives us four of his titles here. What are they?

There are many other hints in the Old Testament; eg Zechariah 2:8-10 where one 'Jehovah' is sent by 'Jehovah'.

From the clues of the Old Testament, we move to the clarity of the New. John begins and ends his Gospel with unambiguous statements about the full divinity of Jesus Christ.

In the prologue, he describes Jesus as *the Word*. We express ourselves most clearly by words and Jesus is the fullest expression of God.

 Read John 1:1

In this verse what three things do we learn about Jesus the Word?

John closes with Thomas' great confession of Christ as *my Lord and my God! (John 20:28)*. And so as to leave us in no doubt that this is the appropriate response to him, Jesus congratulates Thomas on believing. However, at the same time, he also promises greater blessing for those who believe him to be Lord and God without the benefit of seeing him alive.

Jesus promises that when he left his disciples, someone else would come to take his place.

 Read John 14:16-18

How is the Holy Spirit introduced by Jesus to his disciples?

Although the Spirit is *another* – the Greek word means another of the same type – Jesus says, *I will come to you (v 18)*. Again, we see the persons of the

Trinity at work. In this case Jesus and the Holy Spirit are the same, yet different. We know that the disciples received the Holy Spirit at Pentecost. He was so much like Jesus that the disciples knew he was, and is, also divine – anything less would have been a great disappointment.

Read Acts 5:1-6

By comparing verses 3 and 4, how can you show that the Holy Spirit is God?

There are many Scriptures that show that Jesus and the Holy Spirit are of one nature with God. The Jews usually addressed God as The LORD. They did this because they felt that his name, Yahweh (in English, Jehovah), was too holy to take on their lips. But many things that are said of the Lord, Jehovah, in the Old Testament, are said of the Lord, Jesus, in the New. Let's take one example, though you may be able to think of many others.

Read Isaiah 45:23 and Philippians 2:10-11

What is said of God in Isaiah 45:23, which is said of Jesus in Philippians 2:10-11?

THINK IT THROUGH

1. Why is it appropriate for God's goal to be his glory (indeed anything else would be a disaster!) when it is wrong for our goal to be our glory?
2. How would you answer your friendly neighbourhood Jehovah's Witness when he points out to you that the word Trinity is not found in the Bible?
3. What are the implications for our worship of God being one and God being Spirit? See Deuteronomy 6:4-5 and John 4:24.
4. Complete the table overleaf to show how each member of the Godhead was or is involved with every major action of God.

FOLLOW IT UP

1. Think of the ministry God has given you. How do you seek to bring glory to God through it? Are any changes in order in your attitudes, aims or activities?
2. Find as many reasons as you can for gaining a good grasp of doctrine. Share these in your session as a brainstorming exercise. (You may also like to ask whether there are possible dangers and how to counteract these.)

UNIT 2.1

Act of God	Reference(s)	Father	Son	Spirit
Creation	Gen 1:1-3, Col 1:16			
Incarnation – the Coming of Christ into the world as a man	Luke 1:35			
Atonement – Jesus' death on the cross for his people	Heb 9:14			
Resurrection	Rom 1:4 Eph 1:19-20			
Salvation	1 Pet 1:2			
Christian living	2 Cor 13:14			

UNIT 2.2
GOD

His character

God the blessed and only Ruler, the King of Kings and Lord of Lords, who alone is immortal and who lives in unapproachable light, whom no one has seen or can see. To him be honour and might for ever. **1 Timothy 6 :15-16**

IN HIS great book, The Knowledge of the Holy, A.W. Tozer wrote in 1961 of 'a shocking disrespect for the person of God'. Yet things considered blasphemous in Tozer's day now no longer turn a hair. This was highlighted recently when a Kuwaiti newspaper editor was jailed for six months for printing a 'joke' about Adam and Eve. (Q. – Why were Adam and Eve evicted from the garden? A. – Because they wouldn't pay their rent!) If that is one extreme, we seem to have lost all respect for the sacred, not only in society but even in the church where there is little awe of God or sense of his glory.

We need to spend time in biblical reflection on God. Getting to know him will lead us on to wholehearted worship and holy living.

UNIT 2.2

A. SOVEREIGNTY

God's **sovereignty** means that he rules – absolutely. If he did not, he would not be God. Although this has sometimes been challenged philosophically, biblically it is unarguable. See Psalm 115:3. One of the great words used of God over and over again in the book of Revelation is the Greek *pantokrator*, which means all-Sovereign... ruler of the universe. See Revelation 1:8; 4:8.

Read Psalm 99

1. What does this psalm declare about God? (The cherubim are powerful angels in heaven).
2. What is the right response of people on earth to this God? See verses 3 and 5.

For God to be Sovereign, certain other things must be true of him. He must be all-knowing, in all places at all times and all-powerful.

Read the following verses:
- Psalm 90:2
- Jeremiah 23:24
- James 1:17
- 1 John 3:20
- Revelation 19:1

Which particular attribute of God is referred to in each of the above verses?

The truth that God is in control can give us problems when we look at the world. Nevertheless, if God were not in control that would give us many more problems. We would then be at the mercy of the forces of fate, chance and evil.

The whole book of Job deals with the issue of unjust suffering, and if this is a particular problem to you, you might like to do a personal study of this great book – see the Understanding the Bible Track, Unit 1.5, Wisdom. Remember that Satan, who afflicts Job, is always on a lead held by God, even though this lead is an extending one.

The FIEC doctrinal basis singles out four of the many perfect attributes of God when it states...

God is unchangeable in his holiness, justice, wisdom and love.

B. HOLINESS

On the old British passport was a space for distinguishing characteristics. It was difficult to know quite what you were supposed to put. But God's distinguishing characteristic is that he is holy. The Hebrew word translated *holy* originally meant *different*. This idea of *other-ness* sums up everything about him.

Read Isaiah 40:25

God is holy in that he is set apart from everyone and everything else. In relation to us human beings, it is perhaps his moral perfection which sets him apart so completely from us.

Centuries before Christ came, the prophet Isaiah had a vision of the holiness of God.

Read Isaiah 6:1-7

1. What did Isaiah experience both with his senses and his emotions?
2. What was Isaiah's reaction to this encounter with the Holy One?

C. JUSTICE

Aspects of God's holiness include his righteousness and justice. Righteousness is a very beautiful thing, often confused with self-righteousness, which is a very ugly thing. True righteousness involves good, strong, faithful and just relationships, undamaged by sin.

Read Deuteronomy 32:4

1. What is it about God that caused Moses to praise him and attribute greatness to him?
2. Why is this something for which we should truly praise God?

We all have an inbuilt sense of right and wrong because we are made in the image of a just God, even though this image has been shattered by the Fall. God's justice is reflected in his Law – the Ten Commandments (Exodus 20:1-17). These are not arbitrary rules, they are an expression of the character and will of God.

Because God is just, he will not let anyone get away with injustice or unrighteousness. He will judge every single human being for everything they have done (Revelation 20:11-12).

D. WISDOM

Read the following passages of Scripture:
- Psalm 40:5
- Psalm 104:24; Jeremiah 51; 15
- 1 Corinthians 1:22-25
- Ephesians 3:10

UNIT 2.2

 How is God's wisdom demonstrated?

E. LOVE

There are two great statements about God in the first letter of John...
- God is light (1:5)
- God is love (4:8)

This is his nature, and these two qualities are not in opposition, as though God had a split personality. It is because a mother loves that she hates the threat of illness or those who would harm her child. It is because God loves that he hates the sin that threatens to destroy us. Yet love and anger are not equal in the nature of God. God certainly is angry (see Psalm 7:11, Romans 1:18) but he is not anger. God is loving – and he is love. Before he had a sin to hate he had a Son to love.

 Read Deuteronomy 7:7-8

 Why does God love his people?

This is what the Bible means by God's grace – his free, totally undeserved love and goodness.

 Read the following passages:
- Ephesians 1:4c-5
- Romans 5:8
- Titus 3:4-5

 How has God shown and proved his love for his people?

Notice how the New Testament rarely speaks of the love of God without referring to the cross of Christ.

F. FATHERHOOD

The Bible recognises that we are all *God's offspring* (Acts 17:27-28). However, that is not to say we are his sons and daughters by birth. Although we are made in his image, we did not have his nature when we were born. But the staggering truth is that God decided to adopt a vast number of children.

 Look at Galatians 3:26 - 4:7

 List some of the privileges of being adopted into his family from verses 1-7.

When we think of God as Father we should not think that human fathers are the original and that his fatherhood is somehow metaphorical. To judge his fatherhood by our 'dad' can be especially damaging if we have had a bad father ourselves. God is the original, perfect Father. (See Ephesians 3:14-15 NIV margin). Of course, being the perfect parent, he is very interested in our upbringing in the Christian life. He wants us to grow up and not just grow old as Christians.

This involves not only the sense of love and security within his family, but also discipline (Hebrews 12:4-13).

THINK IT THROUGH

1. It could be said of our own time as much as Paul said it of first century Athens, that God is the 'unknown God' (Acts 17:23). How does the true God, who reveals his character in the pages of Scripture, compare with the ideas and images of God that people in our society have? Illustrate your answer from what you used to think God was like and things that you have heard people say about him. What was Paul's response to the ignorance in his own day?

2. Have you ever had an experience where you were very aware of the holiness of God? What effect did it have on you?

3. Jude writes, keep yourselves in the love of God (Jude 21). How can we do this? What happens when we don't?

FOLLOW IT UP

1. Think of a challenge in your ministry or your church which you are facing now. How does a right understanding of God help you to have a right attitude towards this situation?

2. Reflect on a Sunday sermon.
   - *What was the balance between the doctrinal and the practical?*
   - *What Bible doctrines were communicated by the sermon?*
   - *Was there anything striking about their presentation? Did you learn anything new? Was something especially memorably put or illustrated? How was the doctrine applied?*

UNIT 2.3
THE BIBLE

All Scripture is God-breathed and is useful for teaching, rebuking, correcting and training in righteousness, so that the man of God may be thoroughly equipped for every good work. **2 Timothy 3:16-17**

THE BIBLE is a unique book.
Written at intervals over a space of nearly 1400 years... from Italy in the west to Mesopotamia and possibly Persia in the east, the writers themselves were a heterogeneous number of people, not only separated from each other by hundreds of years and hundreds of miles, but belonging to the most diverse walks of life. In their ranks we have kings, herdsmen, legislators, fishermen, statesmen, courtiers, priests, prophets, a tent-making Rabbi and a Gentile physician... The writings themselves belong to a great variety of literary types. They include history, law (civil, criminal, ethical, ritual, sanitary)... treatises, lyric poetry, parable and allegory, biography, personal correspondence, personal memoirs and diaries, in addition to the distinctively biblical types of prophecy and apocalyptic. For all that, the Bible is not an anthology; there is a unity which binds the whole together. An anthology is compiled by an anthologist, but no anthologist compiled the Bible.

That's how Bible scholar F. F. Bruce points out some of its special characteristics.

The Bible's own claim, endorsed by Jesus as we shall see, is that behind the human authors lies a divine author – it is God's word written.

UNIT 2.3

A. ITS ORIGIN

Read Jeremiah 36:4-6 and 2 Peter 1:20-21

How, according to the Bible, did it come to be written?

Characteristically, God involves human agents to achieve his purposes, with all their diverse (and God-given) personalities. At the same time, in Peter's words, **men spoke from God**. When we speak of the Bible as being inspired, we do not mean this in the same sense as, say, Shakespeare was inspired when he wrote *Hamlet*, but rather that it is **Godbreathed**, as Paul puts it in 2 Timothy 3:16.

B. ITS QUALITIES

Read the following verses:
- Psalm 12:6
- Psalm 119:86
- Psalm 119:96
- Acts 24:14
- Deuteronomy 27:9-10; 1 Corinthians 14:37
- Deuteronomy 4:2; Revelation 22:18-19

List the implications of the divine authorship (inspiration) of Scripture from the above verses. If you can, choose one word to describe the character of Scripture.

From these verses and others, we see that the Bible claims to be, in the words of the FIEC doctrinal basis...

'without error' (inerrant); 'fully reliable' (infallible); 'the final authority' and 'always sufficient'.

C. ITS AUTHORITY

At this point, we are sometimes accused of circular reasoning – why do we believe the Bible to be the absolutely true, trustworthy, authoritative, sufficient word of God? Answer – because it says so. However, this is a problem whatever final authority is appealed to. For example, if someone says that reason and rationality is what they live by and you ask them why, they will 'explain' that that's rational. The trouble with all final authorities is that you can't establish their authority by anything higher!

Christians are people with an authoritative Lord and an authoritative book. Jesus' own attitude to the Bible shows that it is impossible to drive a wedge between them.

Read Matthew 22:29-32 and John 10:34-35

 What is Jesus' attitude to the Hebrew Scriptures we know as the Old Testament?

Even after the resurrection when Jesus is explaining what has happened to him to the couple on the Jerusalem-Emmaus road, he does so straight out of the Old Testament Scriptures (Luke 24:25-27). If anyone had a right to begin the gospel from scratch it was Jesus; instead he gives a Bible study! Even the Old Testament, in the final analysis, is all about Jesus (John 5:39). That's why it should be given such high value and close attention.

When it comes to the New Testament, some Jewish background is helpful. In Jesus' day it was quite normal for a Rabbi to appoint and authorise messengers to convey his teaching. When such a *shaliah* delivered the message, it was taken as coming from the Rabbi himself with no less an authority.

 Look up John 14:26; 15:20 and 16:13-14

 How does Jesus expect the truth about himself to be disseminated following his return to his Father?

So all 39 Old Testament books are accepted by Christ and all 27 New Testament books are commissioned by Christ and are our authority. Together, they constitute the canon of Scripture. That is to say, everything in these books is authoritative and sufficient for us. Other writings may have some value, but they do not share this unique status. As we have seen, the last paragraph of the Bible issues a dire warning for anyone who adds or takes anything from the body of Scripture (Revelation 22:18-19).

D. ITS BENEFITS

Christianity is a revealed religion. That is to say we come to know the truth about God and ourselves not by human discovery but by divine disclosure.

 Read Romans 1:18-20 and 28-32

 What could we know about God if we had no Bible?

As Psalm 19 says, no one can get away from the glory of God. Wherever you are in the world, you only have to lift your head and open your eyes. Yet without the Bible, we would still be in the dark as to how we might know and please him. So God, in his desire for a relationship with us, has lovingly communicated through his word.

UNIT 2.3

 Read Psalm 19:7-11

What benefits does David derive from God's words?

Unlike other religious books – for example the Koran, which tells people what they must **do** to be acceptable to God – the Bible tells us that we can never **do** enough. Amazingly it goes on to tell us that he has **done** it all. The Bible is the *good news about Jesus* (Acts 8:35). Ultimately the Bible doesn't teach us how to swim – it introduces us to the Lifesaver.

Sometimes it is said, 'I find the Bible a very difficult book – there is so much I don't understand.'

 Look up 1 Corinthians 2:10b-16

 The Bible is not an easy book, and unaided we will never understand it. Why not?

Even as Christians, people taught by the Spirit, God expects us to work at our Bible reading – to meditate on (or chew over) what we read. He promises that if we do, he will give us the insight we need (2 Timothy 2:7).

 Look at 1 John 2:27

 Why does every Christian have:
• the right to read the Bible?
• the opportunity to understand it for themselves?

Obviously the Lord Jesus provides his church with gifted Bible teachers to help build us up in our faith (Ephesians 4:11- 16). Even so we must always check out what they say. The Bible is the only book in the world which you can always read in the presence of the author, who will teach you the contents and show you how they apply to your life.

 THINK IT THROUGH

Look back and share some of the times when, and the ways by which, God has spoken to you from the Bible.

 FOLLOW IT UP

Card-carrying evangelicals say that **the Bible alone speaks with final authority and is always sufficient for all matters of belief and practice.** *Think of two issues you face in your ministry now. What Bible principles or precedents are relevant to any decisions you may have to take?*

UNIT 2.4
THE LORD JESUS CHRIST

His person

The Son is the radiance of God's glory and the exact representation of his being, sustaining all things by his powerful word. After he had provided purification for sins, he sat down at the right hand of the Majesty in heaven. **Hebrews 1:3**

THE MILLENNIUM was a reminder that Jesus Christ hit the world with such force that his coming split history into two. Even the atheist thinker and writer, H.G. Wells, conceded: 'I am an historian. I am no believer. But this penniless preacher from Galilee is irresistibly the centre of history.'

He still commands phenomenal interest – having more than 20 times the number of web sites of any other person living or dead. There are many different ways in which people think of Jesus Christ – superstar … revolutionary … guru … channeller of the Christ spirit … prophet or simply role model and moral teacher. Few have a bad word to say about him. A recent article praised his 'intellectual brilliance, heroic quality and uncritical love', but surely, the author remarked, 'it is enough that he is the most extraordinary man born in the last two thousand years and was a great redeemer in his lifetime' without treating him like God? But, as we shall see, if he is not the God-Man there is no Christianity and no salvation.

UNIT 2.4

A. THE HUMANITY OF JESUS CHRIST

The Bible is quite clear that Jesus became and will remain fully human, even though he was not always so.

Read the following verses:
- Luke 2:52
- Matthew 4:1-11
- John 4:6
- John 4:7
- John 11:35
- John 13:21

How is Jesus' humanity seen in these situations?

An early church heresy, Docetism, denied that Jesus was truly human. Some people were saying it just 'seemed' that way. Even today Christians can have problems with the truth of Jesus' full humanity. This is one reason why some Roman Catholics pray to Mary or the saints – they think they'll get more sympathy from them, forgetting that Jesus is our brother. (Hebrews 2:11)

Why is it important that Jesus is 100% human?

Match the verses to the truths. So that…

He can be our Mediator	John 13:14-15
He can be our model of a human being filled with the Holy Spirit	Romans 5:18-19
Human beings can exercise the authority for which they were designed by God	Romans 8:3
He can be our perfect substitute on the cross	Hebrews 2:7, 9
He can entirely sympathise with us whatever we are going through	Hebrews 4:15
He can obey God where Adam and the rest of us have disobeyed	1 Timothy 2:5

Jesus was made like us in every way – except one. Paul chose his words carefully when he wrote of **God sending his Son in the likeness of sinful flesh** (Romans 8:3). If you are going to help people, and not merely sympathise, it is no good being as weak as they are. To rescue a drowning man who cannot swim you've got to get into the water with him. It is also rather important that you are able to swim, to life-saving standards.

Read John 8:29,46 and 1 Peter 2:22

Who testified to Jesus' moral perfection when he was living on earth?

B. THE DEITY OF CHRIST

We have already seen how John begins and ends his Gospel by two great assertions of the deity of Christ (see UNIT 2.1). There is no doubt in his mind that Jesus is fully God.

Read:
- John 8:58
- John 10:30-33
- John 12:39-41

How do the above verses support the idea that Jesus knows he is fully God?

Even then, people sometimes say: 'Jesus never claimed to be the Son of God, did he?' It is true that for the first two years of his public life, Jesus did keep his identity hush-hush. He was working to his Father's timetable and to be too direct would have led to the threat of his premature execution. But in the week before his death he told a very significant story which stunned the crowds. He had just incensed the religious leaders by cleaning up the temple and they demanded to see his warrant.

Read Luke 20:9-18

How does Jesus see himself and his mission (as opposed to any other religious leaders)?

The issue of his authority boiled over when Jesus was put on trial before the Jewish Parliament. Frustrated by the contradictions in the prosecution case, the high priest asked Jesus a direct (and leading) question.

Read Mark 14:60-64

Why does Jesus' answer so incense the high priest? (Remember Exodus 3:14 – a fundamental Jewish Scripture.)

The resurrection is God the Father's verdict that Jesus is not guilty of blasphemy even though he proclaims himself to be the uniquely loved Son of God and the great 'I AM'.

It is essential that Jesus is fully divine…

- so that he can reveal God to us. By seeing him we see the Father – we know what the character of God is like (John 14:7-9).
- so that he can reconcile us to God. Any finite creature would be incapable of bearing the full penalty for all the sins of those who would believe in him. God is the only one who can save (eg Isaiah 43:11; Titus 3:4-6).

Philippians 2:5-11 is a magnificent poem on the person of Jesus Christ. Whether Paul composed it himself or quoted it from a very early worship song, there is no doubting how the Bible or the very first Christians view Jesus. This passage traces the person and life of Christ in the shape of a parabola, starting at Infinity, plunging to the very depths and then sharply rising to Infinity – the 'very highest place'.

Read Philippians 2:5-11

1. Fill in the boxes in the chart to show the stages of the life of Christ.

Stages of the life of Christ

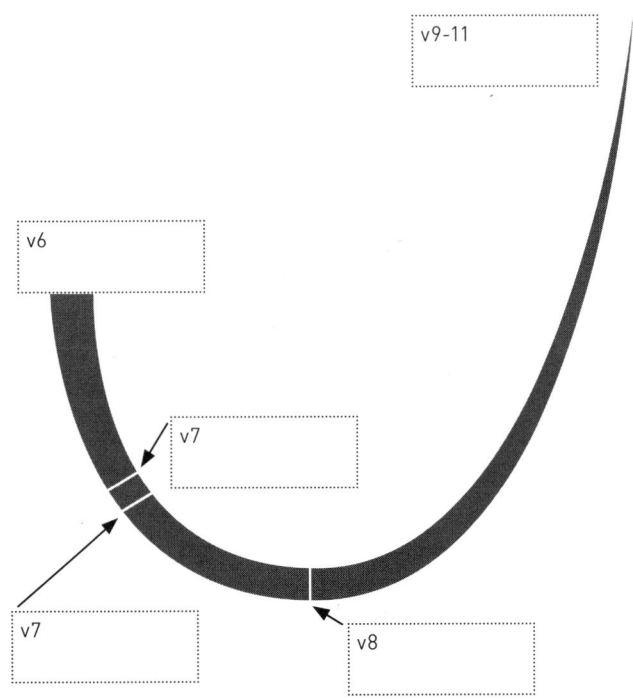

UNIT 2.4

2. Look at verses 5-8. What is the attitude of Christ which we are meant to emulate? Paul writes that 'he emptied himself ' [NIV 'He made himself nothing'] (v7).

3. What does this involve? Although theologians have often read into the passage rather more than is there, the answer is really given to us in the text.

There are big issues here. A child asked recently: 'If Jesus is God, does he know everything'? We know at least one thing he didn't know on earth (Mark 13:32), so the best answer to the question is, 'Yes, apart from the things he chose not to know as a man'.

Christ remains 100% God whilst becoming 100% man. One analogy from the physical world, admittedly imperfect, is light. Light has been discovered to possess properties both of waves and particles, acting contrary in some ways but still being light. Certainly to have the two natures in one person is beyond our full understanding. But there are many things we don't fully understand which are nonetheless true.

Look at verses 9-11. What does it mean that 'Jesus is Lord'?

THINK IT THROUGH

1. There are many ways in which the Bible thinks of Jesus Christ: he has 250 names and titles, together creating a magnificent portrait. Think of some of them now.

2. What are some of the things that are so attractive about the character of Jesus? What would you most like to emulate?

FOLLOW IT UP

Towards the end of the first century, the outlook for the church seemed bleak. The only surviving apostle was an old man, banished to a Roman prison colony. The churches he pastored were coming under the influence of alien teaching, some of which led to serious sexual immorality. Dark clouds of persecution were gathering in the western sky. God's answer is to give a revelation of his Son to the churches via John who saw Jesus, as it were, on a walkabout to inspect and inspire them.

• Spend some time meditating on the description of Jesus in Revelation 1:12-16.
• You might like to pray, submitting your ministry to him for inspection.
• How does a right view of Jesus as he is now inspire us for future ministry?

UNIT 2.5
THE LORD JESUS CHRIST

His death

For Christ died for sins once for all, the righteous for the unrighteous, to bring you to God. **1 Peter 3:18**

THE GREAT SYMBOL of Christianity is the cross – surprising when you consider that, rather than a piece of jewellery, it was the barbaric means of executing the founder of the Faith. The Bible itself emphasises Jesus' death – manifestly the most famous death in history. When we think of William Shakespeare, Florence Nightingale or Sir Winston Churchill, it is not their deaths but their lives that we remember most. Paul, however, writing to the young church he planted at Corinth, reflects, I determined to know nothing while I was with you except Christ and him crucified (1 Corinthians 2:2). At the same time, he is well aware that to the world at large this message is folly.

The Gospels – our 'biographies' of Jesus – give a third of their pages to describe the events surrounding his death. Mark, for example, starts like an express train – straight away he did this… immediately he went there. Then he applies the brakes as Jesus' death draws near.

The great discovery someone makes at or just before

conversion is that Christianity is not what I do in my life to please God, it's all about the death of Jesus on the cross. So let's look at why Jesus' death is so central to our faith, and what it means to all who believe in him.

The weeks leading up to the first Good Friday were the most difficult ones for the disciples. They wanted to go to Jerusalem to kick out the Romans – maybe even to take over the world. But Jesus, almost morbidly, kept referring to his arrest, torture and execution.

Read Mark 10:45

*Jesus knows why he has come to earth. How does he help us to understand the reason for his death? How are we familiar with the idea of **ransom** today?*

By way of preparation, it would be helpful to read through one of the Gospel accounts of the crucifixion – Mark 15, for instance. The killing involves a slow death by suffocation with intense pain in the arms, the legs and the lungs. Jesus shows us in the Gospels how to suffer – he is on the receiving end of terrible injustice, humiliation and unspeakable pain. Any little suffering we go through for being a Christian needs to be seen in the light of the courage, restraint and grace that Jesus exemplifies on the cross (1 Peter 2:21-23; Hebrews 12:2-3).

But if we just had the Gospel accounts, it would be like having the picture without the sound. We would be impressed, but wouldn't be able to make much sense of it all. The Bible writers dwell not on the agony but rather on the achievement of the cross.

Here is an acrostic to help us remember what Jesus achieved by dying on the cross. In the chart draw lines to connect the appropriate verse with each main idea.

C onquest		*Romans 5:6-11*
R econciliation		*1 Peter 3:18*
O ffering		*Colossians 2:14-15*
S ubstitution		*Hebrews 10:11-14*
S alvation		*Galatians 1:3-5*

Let's look at these ideas in a little more detail. They do not give us a total picture, but they cover a vast sweep of the achievement of Christ on our behalf.

A. CONQUEST

Turn back to Colossians 2:14-15

Who and what did Jesus defeat through the cross?

Through the cross Jesus destroyed evil without destroying us, even though we are a party to evil. This is sometimes known as the 'classic' theory of the atonement. It is a glorious part of the work of Christ.

B. RECONCILIATION

Review Romans 5:6-11

1. What does it mean to be reconciled to God?
2. Why do we need to be reconciled?

Related to reconciliation is the concept of *propitiation* – a big word but not longer than say, acceleration. Propitiation is the act of removing someone's anger, in this case God's just anger against our sin. In the NIV it is usually translated 'atoning sacrifice' (Romans 3:25; 1 John 2:2; 4:10), though perhaps the marginal reading – 'Jesus Christ… is the one who turns aside God's wrath' – is clearer. But the scope of the cross is far greater than reconciling individuals here and there to God. The reconciliation achieved by Christ's death is universal (Colossians 1:20). The harmony of the world and the cosmos, ruptured by sin, is re-established through the blood of Christ. The universe is again under its head and peace has been restored.

C. OFFERING

Throughout the Old Testament period people had to be very careful about approaching God. He is holy; we are anything but. Every time the people wanted to pray or to be forgiven, they had to offer sacrifices – morning, noon and night, at special times of the year, like the Day of Atonement, and for specific known sins which they had committed.

Why? A principle was established. Write it down from Hebrews 9:22b.

The word *blood* is used here in a way similar to our use of the word 'bloodshed' – to indicate sudden, violent death. However, the blood of bulls and goats could never really take away sin, because it was not like for like… life for life (Hebrews 10:3-4).

Read Hebrews 10:5-14

How does God - Father and Son - respond to this desperate situation of outstanding evil which could not be got rid of?

Anselm was a godly 11th century Italian, who wrote a treatise on the cross. In his day the popular idea was that God paid the ransom of Jesus' life to the devil who then let all believers go. But Anselm was quite dogmatic that 'God owed nothing to the devil but punishment.' Rather it was the holy character of God, expressed in his Law, that was satisfied at the cross. In the words of an old hymn...

*Because the sinless Saviour died,
my sinful soul is counted free;
For God the just is satisfied
to look on him and pardon me.*

Anselm's critics taught that God could forgive sin just like that; his answer was, 'You have not considered the seriousness of sin', or, we might add, 'the holiness of God'.

D. SUBSTITUTION

The last two doctrines in the acrostic, Substitution and Salvation, are great summary words for how the New Testament views the cross of Christ.

All the New Testament writers look on the cross in this way – Jesus died for us, in our place, bearing our pain and punishment, dying our death.

Read 2 Corinthians 5:21

According to Paul in this verse, what happened on the cross?

Luther called this *the great exchange*. It was he and his fellow Reformers who recovered the prominent biblical doctrine of the cross as penal atonement – ie Christ bore our rightful punishment that we might be forgiven and freed, or *justified* – that is, declared righteous by God.

That word introduces another paradigm (a big picture which controls our thinking) of the cross in the Bible which comes from the law courts – **justification**. To be justified means to be acquitted or, even better than this, to be declared righteous by God through Christ.

Martin Luther and the Reformers, taking their lead from Jesus himself and Paul, were insistent that we are justified by faith alone. We have confidence in Christ and his work on the cross to save us; we contribute nothing. To say we are *justified by faith alone* is the same thing as saying **we are saved by Christ alone**. See John 6:28-29 and Romans 3:21-26; 4:5.

E. SALVATION

The gospel is the greatest real-life rescue story of all time.

Can you think of Old Testament people or groups of people who are rescued and become pictures of the salvation achieved for us by Christ?

 Look up these New Testament references:
- Romans 7:6
- Galatians 1:4
- 1 Thessalonians 5:9-10
- Hebrews 2:14-15
- 1 Peter 1:18
- Revelation 1:5

 What are some of the things from which we are rescued by the work of Christ on the cross?

 THINK IT THROUGH

1. Read Galatians 2:19-20. What does it mean to be 'crucified with Christ'?

2. How does going back to the cross help us when we are:
- discouraged in the service of Christ
- going through a severe trial
- irritated by a fellow-Christian
- feeling that we cannot face God because of something in our life
- elated by some personal success

 FOLLOW IT UP

How can every ministry within a local church directly serve the gospel, the core of which has been set out in this Unit? Briefly review the ministries in which you are involved. Discuss within your group how you can make them more gospel-focused.

UNIT 2.6
THE LORD JESUS CHRIST

His resurrection and reign

Jesus Christ, who is the faithful witness, the firstborn from the dead, and the ruler of the kings of the earth. **Revelation 1:5**

THE RESURRECTION of Jesus Christ is the most momentous event in the history of the world. It makes Christianity unique. All the other founders of world religions are dead. Moslems flock to the burial place of Mohammed in their once-in-a-lifetime pilgrimage to Mecca. People even file past the tomb of Lenin. With Jesus it is different. As the angels at Jesus' tomb said to the women who went to the tomb in the small hours on that first Easter morning – 'Why are you looking for the living among the dead?' (Luke 24.5)

UNIT 2.6

A. THE RESURRECTION – IS IT TRUE?

The evidence has two main strands:
- the tomb where Jesus was buried – the tomb of a well-known, wealthy man – was empty.
- though no account of the actual resurrection is given, many people subsequently saw Jesus alive.

THE EMPTY TOMB

Read Matthew 27:62-28:7

1. Understandably, the chief priests and Pharisees want the tomb secure. Why is it unguarded by both stone and sentries when the women arrive?
2. What discovery do they make when they arrive at the tomb?

Within a couple of months, Peter was preaching to thousands in Jerusalem, the city where it all happened, that Jesus was alive. Yet none of his critics could produce the body.

THE EYEWITNESSES

Jesus appeared to his followers over a period of about six weeks after his resurrection.

Read the following references:
- Matthew 28:8-10
- Luke 24:36-43
- John 20:10-18
- John 20:19-23
- John 20:26-28
- John 21:1-14
- 1 Corinthians 15:3-7 – remember, Paul is writing only 25 years after the event. That is why he can invite his readers to check it out for themselves.

From these references, make a list of those who saw him during this time.

B. THE RESURRECTION – DOES IT MATTER?

Would it really matter if the resurrection were just a 'spiritual' event in the hearts of the disciples rather than a physical event in a tomb in Jerusalem?

Look at the following Bible references, in the diagram below, and then match them, by drawing a line, to the implication which each verse draws from the resurrection.

UNIT 2.6

Luke 24:6-8	It breaks the fear of death
Acts 2:27	It shows that Jesus is ruler of all. He has destroyed all his enemies
Acts 17:31	It shows that Jesus is sinless, the Holy One
Romans 1:4	It confirms the truth of Jesus' words
Romans 4:25	It shows that Jesus has made the once and for all sacrifice for sin
Romans 6:4	It shows that Jesus is the Son of God
1 Corinthians 15:24-26	It gives us faith in God
Hebrews 2:15	It means we can live a new life.
Hebrews 10:12-13	It shows that God will judge the world through Jesus
1 Peter 1:3	It shows that Jesus can justify us (declare us free from sin's penalty)
1 Peter 1:21	It gives us great hope in this life

C. JESUS' TRIUMPHANT ASCENSION

The victorious ascension of Jesus and his triumphant welcome back into heaven was foreseen in the Old Testament. Read Psalm 110. The psalm pictures the coronation of a victorious king returning home from battle. It is actually the most quoted Old Testament Scripture in the New Testament. Peter refers to it in his Pentecost sermon.

Look at Acts 2:33 and John 16:5-8

What does the exaltation of Jesus make way for? Can you trace the connection?

Look again at Acts 2:32-36

UNIT 2.6

What does the resurrection and ascension of Jesus prove?

Read Hebrews 1:3

What is the significance of Jesus' sitting down?

He shares the throne of his Father. That is why in Revelation (22:1-3) we read of the throne (singular) of God and of the Lamb.

What are the implications of the reign of Christ in the heavens for the church of Christ in the world? See:
- *Matthew 28:19-20*
- *Ephesians 4:8-13*

We need to proclaim that Christ is Lord as a matter of urgency and also to live as though Christ is the Master of all things. Jesus tells his disciples who are naturally heartbroken that he is leaving them, that it is better that he returns to his Father:
- so that he can take the highest seat of power in the universe;
- so that he can send his powerful Holy Spirit to be with them in all places and at all times;
- because the ministry he is undertaking for us now requires him to be there. His presence in the Holiest is a perpetual and effective presentation before God of the Sacrifice once offered.

Look at Hebrews 4:14 – 5:6; 7:24-26

How is Christ perfectly qualified to be our priest – that is to say our representative and mediator before God, the one who pleads on our behalf?

THINK IT THROUGH

1. What convinced you Jesus is alive?

2. What bearing does the fact of Christ glorified, seated at the right hand of God, releasing the Holy Spirit and praying for his church have on your life and ministry?

3. What deters us from sharing the good news of Jesus and the resurrection? (Acts 17:18) How can we be more active in sharing this good news?

FOLLOW IT UP

Interview two church members on the person and work of Christ, preferably one who has been a Christian less than five years and one who has been a Christian

UNIT 2.6

more than 10 years. Make it clear that this is not an exam and keep it friendly. Try not to play the expert. Ask:
- *how Jesus' humanity is demonstrated through the gospel*
- *how they would show a Jehovah's Witness for example, from the Bible, that Jesus is divine*
- *whether they can explain how Jesus' death on the cross means that we can be forgiven*
- *what Jesus is doing now*

Review the answers you received. Did anything surprise you? What do the answers suggest about the theological understanding of church members?

UNIT 2.7
THE HOLY SPIRIT

But you will receive power when the Holy Spirit comes on you; and you will be my witnesses in Jerusalem, and in all Judea and Samaria, and to the ends of the earth. **Acts 1:8**

IT IS VERY EASY to fall into one of two equal and opposite dangers when we come to the Holy Spirit. One is to ignore him. It has been suggested that if he were to withdraw from our churches, 95% of our ministries would carry on as they are and we wouldn't notice the difference. The Apostle Paul tells us to live by the Spirit and to be led by him both individually and corporately (Galatians 5:16, 25). The other danger is to become obsessed by him and the spectacular things others may attribute to him. We may then 'lose the plot' of the gospel, glory and grace of our Lord Jesus Christ. In UNIT 2.1 we saw that:
- the Holy Spirit is fully God
- he was playing an active role in all of the major acts of the great drama of God's creation and salvation of the world. He is God-in-action, or, the go-between God. We live in 'the age of the Spirit' – the era marked by his despatch from heaven to glorify Christ and to apply his work of salvation.

UNIT 2.7

A. HIS CHARACTER

It is not easy for us to think of, and impossible to visualise, the Holy Spirit. So to help us we are given pictures of the Holy Spirit at work. Against each reference fill in the substance that the Holy Spirit's work is like. What do we learn about the Spirit in each case?

• 1 Samuel 16:13 _____

• John 1:32-3 _____

• John 3:8/Acts 2:2-3 _____

• John 7:37-39 _____

Yet the Holy Spirit is most definitely a person, not just a power. He can:
• be lied to (Acts 5:3)
• be offended (Ephesians 4:30)
• help us (Romans 8:26)
• pray for us even in groans (Romans 8:26-27)
• as it were, 'whisper in our ear' (Acts 8:29).

We can see something of his character by the titles he is given. Fill in the gaps:

• John 16:13 – the Spirit of _____

• Romans 1:4 – the Spirit of _____

• Romans 8:9 – the Spirit of _____

• Acts 16:7 – the Spirit of _____

B. HIS WORK IN THE WORLD

In both the Old and New Testaments, the word for spirit is the same as that for breath. Sometimes it is difficult to know how the Hebrew (*ruach*) should be translated. The Spirit or Breath of God is the agent of God. Throughout the Old Testament era, he comes and goes. One of the glories of the New Covenant is that he has come to stay.

Read John 16:5-15, the words of Jesus in which he promised that when he had physically gone from the disciples, the Spirit would come.

What is the Holy Spirit's goal in the world? See verses 14-15.

UNIT 2.7

The Holy Spirit doesn't seek to be in the limelight – but he does want glory, attention and adulation for Christ. J.I. Packer, author of the book Knowing God, has likened the Holy Spirit's role to that of a heavenly matchmaker – forging the unlikely match between unattractive sinners and a lovely Saviour.

Look at John 16:8-11

What, according to Jesus, does the Holy Spirit do first, and rather unexpectedly, in the world?

This of course is just what happened when God poured out his Spirit at the first Pentecost. Often the first signs that the Holy Spirit is at work in someone is not that they feel better about themselves – indeed quite the reverse. Mercifully he does not leave us 'stewing.' After showing us what we are like and peeling away our layers of self-esteem like an onion, he shows us Jesus.

NOTE:
The word Parakletos verse 7 (also John 14:16, 26; 15:26) translated counsellor, really means one who draws alongside to help: a supporter, adviser, facilitator, strengthener or the friend-at-court of a bygone age (someone who would put in a good word for you and help you defend yourself if you couldn't afford a lawyer).

C. HIS WORK IN THE CHRISTIAN

Birth. Read the night-time conversation between Jesus and Nicodemus in John 3:3-8, 14-15. We hear a lot today about being born again. Adverts and headlines talk about born again bands (that is to say those who have made a comeback) and brands (eg the VW Golf). A large percentage of the American population claim to be born again. But it is doubtful whether many people have any more idea about what being born again means than poor old confused Nicodemus.

According to Jesus, how is someone born again?

So there is an unseen divine operation as well as a human response to Jesus and his being lifted on the cross.

Growth. Some people seem to think of the Holy Spirit as giving us a kick-start in the Christian life, and then handing over to us. But we need him all the way through. We simply cannot do anything that glorifies God or helps other people without him.

Look at the following Scriptures and take a few minutes to do a biblical brainstorm of the multifaceted ministry of the Holy Spirit to believers.

UNIT 2.7

- Luke 12:11-12
- Ephesians 1;17, 2:22, 3:14-19, 4:3, 5:18-20
- Romans 8:5-16, 15:17-19
- 1 Corinthians 12:1-11
- Philippians 3:3
- 2 Corinthians 3:17-18
- 1 Thessalonians 1:5
- Galatians 5:16-18, 22-23
- 1 John 4:12-13

NOTE:
Since the 1960s, the expression baptism in/of the Holy Spirit has become the subject of some controversy. Some people testify to the tremendous difference a postconversion experience they call the baptism of the Spirit has made to their Christian lives, and then seek to urge this on everyone else. Others say that all Christians are baptised with the Spirit when they are converted. 1 Corinthians 12:13 is a key verse, which like every other verse in the Bible needs to be read in the light of both its immediate context – the section of the letter – and the Bible as a whole.

Two questions which need to be resolved are: Should it be translated 'baptised by one Spirit' or 'in one Spirit' (grammatically, it could be either)? Is this baptism by/in the Spirit (a) an objective act which happened not only to all the Corinthians but all born-again Christians or (b) primarily a deeply felt experience? Either way, it appears that this Holy Spirit baptism happened as part of their conversion, not as a second one-off experience; and that the danger is that we become self-satisfied, for we all need to go on being filled with the Spirit (Ephesians 5:18). We should add that in the early church when new Christians received the Holy Spirit, both they and other people certainly knew about it (eg Acts 10:44-46; Titus 3:4-7).

You should have quite a list! The Holy Spirit draws alongside to help in every area of our Christian lives – praise, witness, service, fellowship, understanding, prayer, preaching, assurance, relationship with God, Christ-likeness. The last is perhaps especially important. He is, as a Puritan called him, the beautifier of souls and produces his fruit (singular in the Greek – one fruit; nine flavours) in our lives (Galatians 5:22-23).

D HIS WORK IN THE CHURCH

The work of the Holy Spirit in Christians spills over into his work in the church. We are meant to grow up in families – with brothers and sisters in local churches.

Read Ephesians 4:3

What does this verse tell us about the Spirit and the unity of the local church?

UNIT 2.7

Read 1 Corinthians 12:4-11

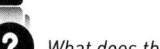

What does this verse tell us about the Spirit and the diversity of the local church?

THINK IT THROUGH

1. How may we go on being filled with the Spirit (Ephesians 5:18)? See the following passages:
- Luke 11:13
- John 7:37-39
- Acts 2:38
- Acts 5:32.

2. Jesus said that the Holy Spirit would bring glory to him – remember John 16:14. How does this help us to evaluate the things that happen in churches, celebrations, conventions etc today?

FOLLOW IT UP

In your area of ministry what spiritual gifts can you identify in the team? Are these gifts being effectively used? Are there other gifts that you should be praying for and looking out for in the church?

NOTE:

The issue of gifts of the Spirit has also been the subject of debate (and alas sometimes worse) since the 'Charismatic Renewal movement'. Some hold that certain revelatory gifts ceased with the end of the Apostolic era, so we would not expect tongues today, to which they might add prophecy and even healing as this is presented in the Scriptures as being a confirmation of Apostolic authority (see 2 Corinthians 12:12). Others would say that there is no indication in Scripture that any of the gifts of the New Testament church would cease until the return of Christ. According to 1 Corinthians 13:10 we can expect the cessation of these gifts when perfection comes, when as Paul says, we shall see face to face. This famous chapter is itself written in the context of the use of gifts in the local church and stresses that love is supreme.

UNIT 2.8

THE HUMAN RACE

Know that the LORD is God. It is he who made us, and we are his; we are his people, the sheep of his pasture. **Psalm 100:3**

TODAY'S HUMANS are a bit schizophrenic when it comes to our identity. On the one hand New Age tells us we are to be gods, deciding what is right and wrong and taking the attitude: 'It's my life!'. On the other hand, Evolutionism has us down as well-developed primates, essentially no different from the animals. As the FIEC's *Light for Life* (commentary on the statement of faith) rightly observes: 'The Bible presents us with a ... radical view of humanity which is unlike that of any other religion or philosophy'. Perhaps the first thing which needs to be said today is that we are creatures. The oldest temptation in the book is for human beings to want to be like God. Our lives are not our own, but belong to the One who made us (Psalm 100:3). This has far reaching implications for the way we live our lives, decide what is right and wrong, etc. The second thing is that all men and women are created in the image of God. The Bible teaches that the first man was *born* as the son of God (Luke 3:38) with great dignity, but you don't need to read the gutter press to realise that we have now fallen. Thank God that is not the end of the story!

UNIT 2.8

A. MANKIND AS DESIGNED – THE DIGNITY OF MAN

Genesis means 'beginnings' and in the first eleven chapters of Genesis, which are an overture to the whole Bible, we discover the beginnings of matter, the solar system, life, the human race, marriage, sex, family, work, sin, agriculture, urbanisation, arts, music, science, languages, religion and God's dealings with men and women. A complex instrument will function best if it is operated as it was originally designed to do. This is especially true with human beings.

Read the following verses in Genesis:
- *1:26-27*
- *1:28*
- *1:27;*
- *2:21-23*
- *2:7*
- *2:15*
- *2:16-17*
- *2:25*

What can we learn about ourselves in the opening chapters of Genesis from the listed verses?

The Bible insists that we all come from the first human parents (Acts 17:26). What are the implications of this?

And though we are jumping ahead of ourselves slightly, have a look at Romans 5:12

Read Psalm 8

The composer of Psalm 8 couldn't get over the dignity that God had given to the human race. What rank has God given to man?

B. FALLEN HUMANITY – THE DEPRAVITY OF MAN

'Man was born free but everywhere he is in chains'. It is difficult to dispute this verdict of the French philosopher, Rousseau. So what is wrong with the human race? Marxists blame the capitalist system which, they say, separates (or alienates) the workers from their finished product and its reward. Humanists, who believe in the essential goodness of man, blame ignorance and believe that given a higher standard of universal education, all will be well. But revolutionary Marxism just replaces one corrupt system with another, and Spurgeon's observation that if you educate devils, all you get is clever devils, still applies. Many other reasons are offered to account for the wrongs of the world. For instance, Existentialists say that life is pointless anyway, and man cannot come to terms with this – hence his problems. But the Bible has a very different diagnosis of our problems.

By the time God created the material universe, evil had already got a hold in his spiritual creation. Evil did not start with man. There had already been a rebellion against God in the spiritual realm, of which there may be a hint in Isaiah 14:12-13. In the story Jesus tells of the wheat and the tares, the farm-labourers are shocked to discover the menacing weeds growing with the corn and wonder how they could have got there. The owner knows – an enemy did this (Matthew 13:28). Jesus identifies the enemy as the devil. It is Satan who brought evil down to earth.

Read how he did this in Genesis 3:1-7 and Genesis 2:16-17

Compare Genesis 2:16-17 with Genesis 3:1, 4. How did Satan twist the words of God to Adam and Eve?

Tragically, in one sense it was just as Satan had said it would be. Their eyes were opened to know the difference between good and evil. Before then man had only known the good, but now he had lost his innocence.

Read Genesis 3:8-24

What were some of the other disastrous consequences of the Fall of mankind? (from the following verses):
- 8-10
- 16
- 17-19
- 23-24

Look at Mark 7:21-23

What was Jesus' diagnosis of the human problem?

You can see that this explains a lot. When theologians talk about the *total depravity* of the human race, they don't mean we are totally depraved. If you put a drop of cyanide in a drink, the liquid is not 100% cyanide, but it is 100% poison. So with humanity and sin, everything about us is affected by this rebellion against God – our emotions, our thinking, our behaviour, our work, our impact on the environment and our relationships with others and with God. Our rebellion not only causes us a lot of problems. More seriously, it puts us in big trouble with God and makes us liable to his judgement (Ephesians 2:3).

UNIT 2.8

C. NEW MAN – MANKIND IN CHRIST

Remember what David wrote about man in Psalm 8 – *You have put everything under his feet.* That's us! At the moment, as the writer to the Hebrews recognises, it doesn't look this way. We humans have forfeited our high position by our rebellion. The amazing thing is that God planned to restore this position to members of the human race, has acted decisively to do so and even now is in the restoration process, as the writer to the Hebrews rejoices.

Read Hebrews 2:5-17

1. What was Jesus made and why? (v9)
2. What is Jesus' position now? (v9)
3. How does this gloriously affect us? (vv14-15)

The tremendous dignity that God has given to mankind can be summarised from this passage...
- The Son of God became man, a member of the human race (vv8-9, 14)
- There is a man in the glory of heaven (vv9, 11)
- He will lead many other human beings to heaven (v10)
- Jesus is not ashamed to call these men his brothers ... family (v11)

One of Paul's favourite little expressions to describe the life of the Christian is *in Christ*. He uses it 164 times in his letters. We were *in Adam* – descended from him and inheriting his character. When we are born again we are *in Christ* – a member of his race, enjoying his family rank, even sharing a growing family likeness which will be completed in glory.

THINK IT THROUGH

1. The Bible's teaching that we are created in the image of God has huge implications which are often rightly thought of in terms of racism and sexism, or abortion and euthanasia. But what are the implications of this truth for life in the local church? See, for example, James 3:9-12. What are the special temptations for leaders in this area?
2. Like Adam and Eve, we are suckers for temptation. Have you recognised some of Satan's schemes in your experience (2 Corinthians 2:11)? What temptations have you faced in your own particular ministry?

FOLLOW IT UP

Clearly, being human is a vast subject. If you are interested in the question of how many parts we have, everyone agrees we have at least one – a body. Most people, including all Christians, would say that we had at least two. Some Christians would add a third – see Wayne Grudem's Systematic Theology, IVP. On the vexed

UNIT 2.8

question of freewill, the Bible has little directly to say, though its emphasis always seems to be on the freewill of God. D.A. Carson's Divine Sovereignty and Human Responsibility, (Marshall Pickering), is the fullest recent treatment of this subject by an evangelical scholar. Launch out onto the tricky slopes of the gender issue and you will face an avalanche of literature, including Andrew Anderson (Ed.), Men Women and Authority, Serving together in the church, Day One.

Interview two church members on the subject of doctrine:
- *How do they find doctrine – exciting? dry? important?*
- *Are there any Bible doctrines which puzzle or trouble them? Do they have any theological questions?*
- *Are there any gaps in their doctrinal understanding that they are aware of? Issues they would like to be addressed from the pulpit?*
- *Have they ever read any books on doctrine? Were they helpful?*
- *Can they give examples of how they have applied Bible doctrine so that it has been a real help?*

UNIT 2.9

THE CHURCH

Christ loved the church and gave himself up for her to make her holy, cleansing her by the washing with water through the word. **Ephesians 5:25-26**

THE BIBLE is a great love story, ending with the wedding of all time – the marriage feast of the Lord Jesus Christ and his pure, radiant bride, the church. This is rather different from the accepted idea of 'the church', helped along by popular sitcoms or the bitter experience of many who are no longer part of a church. For now, the church of Jesus Christ has many faults (us being among them), and the Bible is as honest as ever when it paints the early churches 'warts and all'. Yet Jesus is totally committed to the church. He came not just to 'save private sinners' but to build his church, and he promised that the gates of hell would not stop her advancing (Matthew 16:18). Right around the world we see the phenomenal growth of the church of Jesus Christ – even, indeed especially, in the trouble spots of the world.

UNIT 2.9

A. WHY CHURCH?

Look up Ephesians 3:10, 21

What is the point of the church?

Following on from this, what is the mission of the church by which she may fulfil her raison d'être?

Read Matthew 28:18-20 and 1 Thessalonians 1:8

B. WHAT IS THE CHURCH?

The Greek word ecclesia, translated 'church' in English, started out as an ordinary word meaning a gathering or assembly. For the purposes of this study, it is used in two related ways in the New Testament. What are they?
- *Ephesians 1:22-23*
- *Romans 16:3-5a*

Some people think they can be part of the universal church without being part of a local church. But the local church is simply an outcrop of the universal church – in J.B. Phillips' lovely translation of Philippians 3:20, 'a colony of heaven'. When you see a new crescent moon, you don't say: 'There's a sliver of moon!' You say: 'There's the moon!' So with the local church – it is 'the church', in microcosm admittedly, but still the church. The local church is particularly 'the church' when her members gather for worship, and the ministry of the word and the ordinances (1 Corinthians 11:18).

There are literally dozens of pictures of the church in the New Testament. Brainstorm the ways in which the church is described in the Bible (a few are given in the diagram below).

From the verses given in the diagram below, what picture is given of the church and what does each tell us about the church of Jesus Christ?

From what we've learned so far, attempt a biblical definition of 'the church'.

The church is people … God's people …us. Sometimes people complain – 'Why doesn't the church do something?' – as though the church was a mysterious, impersonal corporation with a remote HQ and board of directors. It is not them or it – it is *us*!

Acts 2:42-47 is a beautiful miniature portrait of the early church

UNIT 2.9

What were core activities? These can act as a check list to our own.

Reference	Picture(s)	Name of Church
1 Corinthians 12:12-13		
Ephesians 5:25-27		
1 Corinthians 3:16-17		
1 Timothy 3:15		
1 Peter 2:9-10		

C. THE ORDINANCES OF THE CHURCH

There are just two simple ceremonies practised in the local church in obedience to the wishes of the Lord Jesus (Matthew 28:19; Luke 22:19-20):
- One is to be baptised, from an ordinary Greek word meaning dipped or even drowned in water, as a mark of entry into faith.
- The other is to remember Jesus in his death by taking bread and wine in Communion or the Lord's Supper. They are acted signs of the gospel, focusing our attention on what Christ has done for us.

See:
- *Acts 22:16*
- *Romans 6:3-4*
- *1 Corinthians 1:13-15*

What is baptism an 'acted sign' of?

Evangelical Christians, taking the Bible as their authority, differ in their understanding and practice of baptism. Is it for infants of Christian families or for believers? How much water should be used? But evangelicals are agreed that only faith in Christ on the believer's part puts him or her into a right relationship with God, and even that faith is the gift of God. No one can be born again by doing anything, including being baptised. The same is true of taking Communion. 'It is good for our hearts to be strengthened by grace, not by ceremonial foods (Hebrews 13:9)'. There is no magic in the bread or wine. At the same time Jesus has given us the Lord's Supper as a means of receiving his grace through faith.

Read 1 Corinthians 10:16-21 and 11:17-29

If you were asked, 'What are you doing when you take Communion?', how would you answer?

Communion is a sign, but less like a blue motorway junction marker than a brown sign welcoming you on arrival to a new place with symbols of the delights of the city. Just as there is something special about sharing a meal with someone, so there is something special about taking bread and wine in Jesus' honour and memory, in his presence and with his people.

D. UNITY IN THE CHURCH

In the New Testament there are many pleas for unity between Christians. Their emphasis is primarily that of unanimity – being of one heart – rather than uniformity, all being the same, or even a united organisation. Many such pleas are addressed to believers comprising local churches, eg Philippians 4:2. Our Father God is very concerned that the children of his family love each other and 'get on'. What is less commonly noted today are the many New Testament pleas for separation. The lovely little letter 2 John is typical.

Read 2 John

The chosen lady (v1) and her chosen sister (v13) are probably churches. John is writing as an apostle from one church to another.

What do we learn about love and unity between Christians?

When is it necessary to distance ourselves from people within churches?

THINK IT THROUGH
We live in a day when the consumer is king, choice is in and commitment is out. What practical and spiritual pressures today make commitment to a local church difficult to sustain?

FOLLOW IT UP
1. What purpose do you think the Lord may have for drawing you with your various personalities, strengths and gifts, together in your local church at this time in history?

2. How can you make your local church the best she can be for the glory of Jesus?

3. Do a house-to-house/street questionnaire survey, along the following lines: Which statement below best describes how you believe the universe came into being?
    a. through the creation of God
    b. through natural chance processes without God
    c. other (please state)
    d. don't know

UNIT 2.9

Which statement below best describes how you view the Bible?
   a. the written word of God
   b. a wise spiritual source book
   c. a collection of outdated stories and commandments
   d. other (please state)

Which statement below do you believe best describes Jesus Christ?
   a. the only Son of God
   b. just a good man
   c. a prophet
   d. a myth/legend
   e. other (please state)

Which statement below do you believe best describes a Christian?
   a. someone who trusts Jesus Christ for forgiveness through his death on the cross
   b. someone who goes to church regularly
   c. someone who tries their best to live a good life
   d. other (please state)
   e. don't know

What statement below best describes what you think happens after a person dies?
   a. I believe that people either go to heaven or hell
   b. I believe that everyone goes to heaven
   c. I believe that people return to earth in another form
   d. I believe there isn't anything after death
   e. other (please state)
   f. don't know

Finally –
If you knew that God would answer any one question of yours, what would you ask?

UNIT 2.10
THE FUTURE

The kingdom of the world has become the kingdom of our Lord and of his Christ, and he will reign for ever and ever. **Revelation 11:15**

IT'S NOT JUST THE OLD who ask the question: 'What is the world coming to?' With global warming, the population explosion, resource depletion, world economic crises, let alone international terrorism, political instability and the nuclear threat, many fear for the future of planet Earth and her peoples. There has always been a longing for Utopia, but, as Lord Acton famously recognised, we human beings cannot handle power without being corrupted. So the announcement of Isaiah, *See, a king will reign in righteousness* (Isaiah 32:1) should have us dancing in the streets. The coming kingdom of this king is one of the great themes of the Bible and of Jesus' own teaching.

UNIT 2.10

A. THE KINGDOM OF GOD

The book of Daniel was written when the little Jewish nation, having flagrantly violated God's laws, had been kicked like a football between the world superpowers vying for supremacy. The Babylonians under Nebuchadnezzar committed many atrocities in overrunning Jerusalem and then deporting most of the survivors to Babylon as slaves. The Babylonians, in turn, were overthrown by the Medo-Persians, the next superpower to appear on the horizon. See Understanding the Bible, Track 1.3, *History*. But despite all this turmoil, it would be wrong to think that God had lost control. He gave Nebuchadnezzar a dream about a magnificent statue with a head of gold working down to feet of clay which represented successive world empires. Then a rock, 'not cut by human hands', was used like a ball in a cosmic bowling alley flattening the statue and pulverising its raw materials.

Read Daniel 2:44-45 and 7:13-14

From these verses what do we learn about the kingdom of God?

Of course, *kingdom of God* and *Son of Man* are both key terms in the teaching of Jesus from the outset of his public life. He proclaims that the kingdom of God is near. This is good news, or gospel, and people should be ready for its arrival.

On one occasion, Jesus is asked the question on everybody's lips – when will the kingdom of God come? See Luke 17:20-30

1. Can you explain his answer? (See also Luke 11:20; 19:11-13)
2. When we pray, 'your kingdom come', as Jesus taught us (Luke 11:2), what are we asking for?

It seems clear that, for Jesus, the kingdom of God has both present and future forms. So the kingdom of God arrives by gradual process until that day, and by sudden crisis on that day when Christ will rule supreme and all rebellion against his rule will be quashed for ever.

B. THE COMING OF CHRIST

The return of the King – the coming of Christ – dominates the horizon of the New Testament. We are to pin all our hope on the grace to be given to us when Jesus Christ is revealed (1 Peter 1:13). Other hopes may well disappoint us. Indeed Paul says that if Christians only had hope for this life, they would be the most pathetic, pitiable people on the face of the earth (1 Corinthians 15:19).

See 1 John 3:2-3

1. As Christians, why should we be so excited by the coming of Jesus? And what effect will this have on our lives now?
2. From the following Scripture references, come up with a series of words which describe the return of the Lord Jesus Christ to this earth:
   - Matthew 24:29-30, 36, 43
   - 1 Thessalonians 4:16
   - 2 Peter 3:10-12
   - Isaiah 33:17

The coming, as it is usually called in the New Testament, has, along with end-time phenomena like the Tribulation and the Antichrist, been the subject of much speculation. Yet in Bible terms, even the first generation of Christians lived in the *last days* (Hebrews 1:2). And it is important that we do not fall into the trap of the nursery rhyme pussy-cat who went up to London to look at the Queen but was fixated by a little mouse. We must keep our eyes on Jesus.

C. THE JUDGEMENT

Jesus will return with a shout loud enough to wake the dead, which is just what will happen (John 5:28-29)! Everyone, alive or dead, will then appear before the bench of Christ.

Read Matthew 7:21-23; 25:31-46 and John 3:35-36

On what basis will everyone be judged?

Read Matthew 22:1-13 – Jesus gives us pictures here of heaven and hell. One man, who was not fit for heaven, was not permitted to stay at the banquet

1. How are heaven and hell described by Jesus in this parable?
2. What do the wedding clothes (v12) stand for?

D. HELL

Many people ask: 'How can a God of love send anyone to hell?' The question the Bible asks, however, is turned around – how can a God of holiness take anyone into heaven? In Romans 3:25-26, Paul poses the question and gives the amazing answer. Nearly everything we know about the awful existence of hell comes from Jesus himself.

Read Mark 9:43-49

The word that Jesus uses three times here for hell is the place-name Gehennah. This was a deep dark ravine just to the south of the city of Jerusalem. It was used as a common grave and a rubbish dump for the city. The fire there never went out. In the Old Testament times, when it was known as the Valley of Hinnom, it had been used for the most appalling occult practices, including child sacrifice.

How should we respond to such terrible teaching? Think of at least two ways.

The tremendous thing is that Jesus took our condemnation so that we never have to suffer hell ourselves.

No wonder Charles Wesley penned these lines:
Love moved him to die, and on this we rely
He has loved, He has loved us, we cannot tell why.
But this we can tell. He has loved us so well,
and has laid down his life to redeem us from hell.

E. HEAVEN

Obviously it is not possible to give a full description of heaven. After all, if you had to describe a seaside town to a Kalahari bushman, you might struggle. How much more difficult to explain the glories of heaven to an earthling. In 2 Corinthians 12:4, Paul says that not only is he not able to describe heaven, but he is not allowed to describe heaven. Heaven now is the place of God's immediate presence but is sometimes called 'the intermediate state' because it is a temporary state of affairs until the Lord Jesus Christ returns in glory. He will raise the dead and judge the world. The Bible then tells us the amazing fact that, having destroyed the old heavens and earth, God is actually coming to live with his own people in a glorious new city. (If you are interested in following this through, see 2 Corinthians 5:1-10; Hebrews 12:22-24; 2 Peter 3:11-13 and Revelation 6:9- 10; 21:1-3). In diagram form the sequence might look like this.

UNIT 2.10

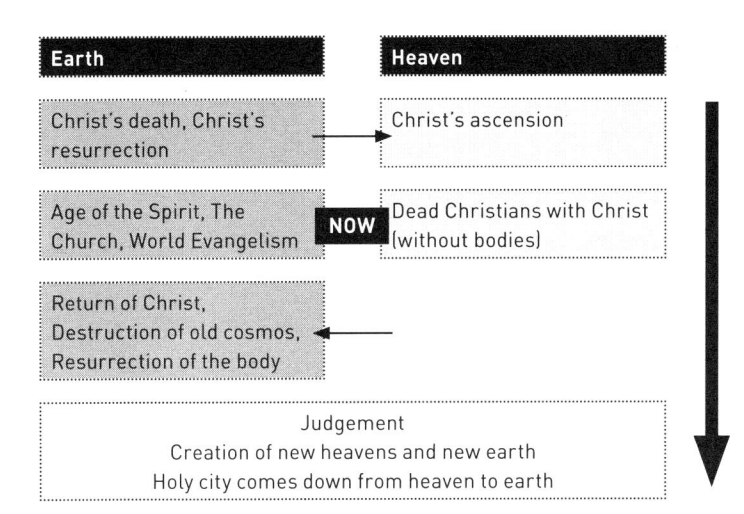

Earth	Heaven
Christ's death, Christ's resurrection	→ Christ's ascension
Age of the Spirit, The Church, World Evangelism **NOW**	Dead Christians with Christ (without bodies)
Return of Christ, Destruction of old cosmos, ← Resurrection of the body	

Judgement
Creation of new heavens and new earth
Holy city comes down from heaven to earth

For his encouragement, John is given a vision of the eternal heavenly city, and told to write about it under the inspiration of the Holy Spirit.

Read his vision in Revelation 21:1-4, 10-27; 22:1-5

It seems that the city descends from heaven and merges with the new earth, but this is beyond our full comprehension.

What will not be there? What will be there instead?

Absent	Present

From Chapter 22:3-5, name three things that heaven's citizens will be doing.

Read Chapter 22:1-2

What is at the centre of heaven?

THINK IT THROUGH

Why don't we think about heaven and hell as much as the early Christians? How can we rectify this?

FOLLOW IT UP

*Paul writes that **the Day** will reveal the quality of our work (1 Corinthians 3:13). How can we ensure the ministry we are involved with now will have eternal value and survive this trial by fire on the day Christ returns? Talk through any danger signs with your tutor, a church leader or a friend.*

BE PREPARED
to serve the LORD

Prepared for Service provides a unique, part-time training opportunity for both men and women with a desire to serve the Lord Jesus Christ and his people, to be better equipped for works of service in local churches, their communities and the world.

It aims to achieve this by:

- Offering an environment where gifts and abilities can be realistically assessed to help understand God's purpose for an individual's life

- Providing a biblically-based training resource to help individuals develop knowledge of God's word within the framework of academic study

- Giving practical and pastoral models helping individuals serve in ways that are appropriate to the contemporary world

- Providing teaching, pastoral care and practical experience for individuals with the support of their local churches

For Information Pack/Application Form, please contact:

The 'PfS' Administrators
25, Felton Road,
Poole, Dorset. BH14 0QR

Tel: 01202 738416
Email: pfs@fiec.org.uk
Web: www.fiec.org.uk

PREPARED FOR SERVICE

A Training Ministry of
The Fellowship of Independent Evangelical Churches

FIEC — Bible churches together

Could PfS fulfil your needs in serving the LORD?

Continue your studies at home with the
Open Bible Institute
— a thoroughly Bible-centred, distance-learning college

One of the great seats of learning

- **Short Courses in ministry skills:** 10-session courses in Administration, Christian Mission & Ministry, Pastoral Care, Preaching and Youth & Children's Work.

- **The Moore College Correspondence Course:** a great course encompassing biblical studies, church history, doctrine, apologetics and ethics.

- **Certificates of Higher Education:** fully validated qualifications in 'Biblical Studies and Theology' and 'Biblical Studies and Ministry' equivalent to the first year of a degree.

For an information pack or an informal discussion, please contact:
0845 225 0885
admin@open-bible-institute.org
www.open-bible-institute.org

open bible institute

NOTES

Certification

If you would like your work to be assessed by an independent organisation then please send a clearly named folder containing answers to all the exercises in the this book to the Open Bible Institute:

The Open Bible Institute
Elm House
37 Elm Road
New Malden
Surrey KT3 3HB, UK

A marking fee is payable. For full details please see the website:
www.open-bible-institute.org/learn2lead

Authors

Learn2Lead was developed by:
Brian Boley
Richard Underwood
Paul Mallard
Dr Ray Evans
Tim Saunders